Pearls of Wisdom
FOR EVERYDAY
LIVING

BY

Precisus L. Curry

Copyright 2020 © Precisus L. Curry
Scriptures taken from the New King James Version, Copyright © 1982 by Thomas Nelson, Inc. Used by permission. All rights reserved.

Published by:
EMPOWER ME BOOKS, INC.
A Subsidiary of Empower Me Enterprises, Inc.
P.O. Box 16153 Durham, North Carolina 27704 www.EmpowerMeBooks.com

All Rights Reserved. No part of this book may be reproduced, stored in a retrieval system, or transmitted in any form or by any means, electronic, mechanical, photocopying, recording, scanning, or otherwise, without the prior written permission of the publisher.

ISBN: 978-1732773134
Printed in The United States of America

Pearls of Wisdom
FOR EVERYDAY LIVING

*~ In Loving Memory ~
of my daughter,
Anissa 'Nissy' Barbee*

I dedicate this to…

My loving husband, Michael who has been both supportive and helpful during this time.

*My daughter Anissa, my son Larry Jr.,
My grandson Larry III
Also to my Sisters and my Brother.*

Bishop Marion E. Wright, Sr., my Pastor, I would like to thank you for your knowledge and understanding that God has blessed me with from your teaching and preaching the Word of God. "…And I will give you pastors according to mine heart, which shall feed you with knowledge and understanding." (Jeremiah 3:15)

That special person that helped me get started in writing these inspiring messages every day. He started sending out messages to our list of Prayer Warriors. Somehow, he turned this task over to me in 2012; I then started randomly sending messages out every morning. I received so much feedback from people that they were waiting every morning to read them…. So, thank you my friend, Elder Sylvester Thorpe for letting God use you to get to me. Now I can share these messages in book form, and I do believe that some will be inspired and accept God as their Lord and Savior.

Understanding to achieve anything requires faith and belief in yourself, hard work, determination and encouragers like Renee Foster, Terry Lewis, Stephanie Waters, Shirlene Drew, Betty Thomas. I know now that all things are possible if you believe in yourself and have those few pushers behind you who believe in you as well. Thanks guys!!!

PRAYER

Father,

My help comes from You and You alone, who made heaven and earth. In Your word You say that I am the head and not the tail, I am above and not beneath, I am the lender and not the borrower. I know that whatever I ask in Your name is already done, so Lord, I ask that every seed that I plant let it come with a heart of gratefulness. God, I ask that You put a spirit of praises in my mouth that I can worship You with all my being. Whatever I plant in this season, let it blossom and bloom for my harvest in next season. Your love has never failed me, Lord, so I surrender my heart, dreams, plans, and desires into Your Hands. Lord, I know You have incredible plans for me. If I need to move, move me, and If I need to stay, plant my feet firmly on the ground. Let Your will be made complete in my life. Let all that I do and all that I say glorify Your Name. Thank You for removing the scales from my eyes and thank You for giving me a spiritual ear to hear You.

My heart is so full of love for You!!

In Your Matchless Name, I
pray, Amen.

TABLE OF CONTENTS

Introduction

Section 1	Storm and Solution Pearls	11
Section 2	Pearls of Motivation	48
Section 3	Faith Pearls that Change Doubts into Beliefs	72
Section 4	Pearls of Gratitude	84

About the Author

INTRODUCTION

"I can do all things through Christ who strengthens me."
(Philippians 4: 13 KJV)

I need God in my life every day. From the moment I wake up, I give God a 'Thank You' praise despite what my day will bring, and then I put it all in His hands and trust that He will guide my steps. As I was growing up, I learned about Jesus, but I did not have Jesus in my heart. I now know that as long as I have this gift of a grateful heart, I will always be able to see and appreciate all the blessings that God has bestowed upon me. That is why I would like to share these messages with you that helped me through many of my experiences.

I chose the title "God's Given Pearls of Wisdom for Everyday Living" because I believe that everyone has been in a situation where they needed God's help. A pearl is a beautiful treasure that is the product of an injured life. It is a torn tissue from a wounded oyster that was caused by sand or grit. That is the way I see God's ability to work in me. Taking my imperfections and making them perfect. That is what this book is about the challenges and struggles we encounter daily. The messages in this book will help you in some way to take a look at your situations and to see how God will guide you to Him.

Trust me, my friend, the pain and the struggles are real!! But remember, the struggles you are in today are strengthening you for more incredible blessings if you keep God in your situation. So, do not give up. Do not give in. Surrender to God's will, and he will carry your burdens and make the load so much easier for you. He will comfort you; He will give you peace; joy and will heal where it hurts. He will provide you with an extreme makeover! Trust me; I am talking from experience. He has transformed me. Only God can change you; you cannot do it; His Holy Spirit will.

Let God lead you through your circumstances. Over the years, my Pastor, Bishop Marion E. Wright, Sr., has taught me, "If You Pray Your Day, Before You Live Your Day, You Will Be Successful in Your Day, All Day Long."

Storm and Solution Pearls

II Chronicles 7:14

If my people, which are called by my name, shall humble themselves, and pray, and seek my face, and turn from their wicked ways then will I hear from heaven, and will forgive their sin, and will heal their land.

STORM & SOLUTIONS PEARLS

"In all thy ways acknowledge him, and he shall direct thy paths." - Proverbs 3:6 KJV

Don't stop now!! Your breakthrough is ahead of you. The last mile is usually the hardest one... so keep moving forward and stop looking back, your blessing is ahead. God is about to do something BIG! Continue to believe in God and He will bring victory. Strengthen your Faith to believe that ALL things are possible.

_____

_____

_____

_____

_____

_____

_____

_____

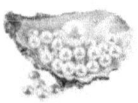

"If my people, which are called by my name, shall humble themselves, and pray, and seek my face, and turn from their wicked ways; then will I hear from heaven, and will forgive their sin, and will heal their land."
II Chronicles 7:14 KJV

We are living in a time that we need to seek God. It's a time where the Church must pray as never before. When you understand what prayer is and how it works, you can see great changes in your life and in your city and nation. Jesus has instilled in us the ability to be great prayer warriors. He has given you His Word and His Spirit. He knows what to give you and what you should pray for to bring change. His mighty word is in you. Prayer unlocks the door to God's solution for every need. Remember: Heartfelt prayers of the righteous availeth much. It is the power of our prayers that will bring peace to our city, state and nation. Saints of God it is praying time!! Prayer is powerful!!

_____

_____

_____

_____

STORM & SOLUTIONS PEARLS

"But as it is written, Eye hath not seen, nor ear heard, neither have entered into the heart of man, the things which God hath prepared for them that love him."
- I Corinthians 2:9 KJV

You have been trying to do some things in your life, but your vision seems blurry. You are not quite sure which way to go or you usually end up at a dead end or doing the same thing the exact same way. Well, God says, it's time to refocus your outlook. Some things have expired and are no longer available through the manufacturer. Stop trying to do things the old way. Stop trying to do things the same way someone else did. God says He has something new for you. New ideas, product, resources, connections, relationships, and ministries. He wants you to refocus your eyes on the new and clearly see the path he has for you.

___
___
___
___
___
___

STORM & SOLUTIONS PEARLS

"For I know the thoughts that I think toward you, saith the Lord, thoughts of peace, and not of evil, to give you an expected end." - Jeremiah 29:11 KJV

Every problem and troubling situation we may face in our life is allowed by God for a special purpose. It is either to perfect us in the place we are now or to move us to the next level. It is something far greater than our current situation. Our Faith is being tested and sharpened to equip us for the battles of this world that we are going to face. The path to victory has already been set in place. There is nothing that can destroy us if our faith is in God even when the darkness of any storm surrounds us. Even though we may still face the attack of the enemy, our victory is still secure in Him. Christ will not abandon us when our situation does not look promising. He knows our weaknesses and has seen our failures, yet His power is more than enough

to take us safely through.

_____

_____

_____

_____

_____

STORM & SOLUTIONS PEARLS

"Being made so much better than the angels, as he hath by inheritance obtained a more excellent name than they." - Hebrews 1:4 KJV

When obstacles come, embrace the challenge and prepare for better!!! Whatever trials you are going through, keep your eyes on Him. God is preparing you for better. He is perfecting His gift in you. And in His timing, he will elevate you. Be thankful for every experience. Remember, take your eyes off the circumstances. Look up; that's where your attention needs to be. He's the only one who can change it. So, prepare yourself for excellence!

_____
_____
_____
_____
_____
_____
_____
_____

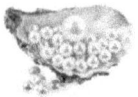

> "God is our refuge and strength, a very present help in trouble. Therefore will not we fear, though the earth be removed, and though the mountains be carried into the midst of the sea; Though the waters thereof roar and be troubled, though the mountains shake with the swelling thereof. Selah." - Psalm 46:1-3 KJV

Hang in there, God loves you, just have faith, wait on the Lord", are some of the things you have been hearing over and over again. Hearing this can become annoying; however, no one wants you to give up more than the enemy. Satan would love nothing better than to have our trials drive us away from God. It could be days, weeks, months, or years of our time before God answers us, but Satan wants us to think God doesn't' care. You must get to the point where you are willing to believe that God has done it. No matter how hopeless it seems, no matter how bad it may look nor how long you have been waiting, you must believe God's promises. Read Your Bible Daily!! Decide that God is Truth and no matter what changes, HE WON'T!! He will never leave you or forsake you. You will witness the change. You will see your miracle. Through all our suffering God uses it for our benefit. Everything we went through was necessary!!!

STORM & SOLUTIONS PEARLS

"Be strong and of a good courage, fear not, nor be afraid of them: for the Lord thy God, he it is that doth go with thee; he will not fail thee, nor forsake thee."
Deuteronomy 31:6 KJV

***"Life isn't about waiting for the storm to pass ...it's about learning to dance in the rain."
– Vivian Greene***

No matter how you feel, get up, pray up, and never give up. Life is not about waiting on the storm to pass. It's about how well you weather the storm. No matter how hard the storm is raging around you, just stand firm, and believe that God will see you through it. But one thing is for certain, when you come out of the storm, you won 't be the same person who walked in. That's what the storm was all about, trusting God.
Now Praise Him!!

_____

_____

_____

_____

"Two are better than one; because they have a good reward for their labour." - Ecclesiastes 4:9 KJV

In this day and time Satan is trying to defeat God's people. Stealing, killing and destroying the lives and minds of God's people is his intention. This is the battle that we, the saints of God, are fighting. We must fight and hold up the arms of each other until the enemy is defeated. For the word of God says we must "pray without ceasing" for we will be victorious if we trust God. Now that the battle is on, hold your arms up for your brethren because they need you and you need them.

> "Wait on the Lord: be of good courage, and he shall strengthen thine heart: wait, I say, on the Lord."
> Psalm 27:14 KJV

Sometimes we find ourselves in such horrible messes that it's hard to imagine what's going to happen next. Have you been praying about a situation in your life and found yourself waiting on a breakthrough? Are you wondering why the answer hasn't come yet? Do you feel as though God is ignoring you? God is only testing your faith.

Other times, when we pray long and hard about a situation in our life without receiving an answer immediately, we start to wonder if God heard our prayers or how long is it going to take to hear from Him. But God does hear your prayers. He wants you to put your trust in Him completely. When people patiently and expectantly wait on God during terrible circumstances, suddenly God breaks through in a way we could've never imagine. Our situations change suddenly without warning. God moves quickly. So, don't give up! Don't stop believing! Stay full of hope and expectation. Keep the faith. Your breakthrough is in His time.

STORM & SOLUTIONS PEARLS

"In all thy ways acknowledge him, and he shall direct thy paths." - Proverbs 3:6 KJV

When we ask God for guidance, He always provides instructions. If you ever question the path you are on or a decision you are making, ask God for guidance. When He gives you the answer, you will know it is right. You must remember ask Him and listen for His instructions. He knows the way and will guide you on how to get there. Don't move forward until you hear the voice of the Lord.

"Trust in the LORD with all thine heart; and lean not unto thine own understanding." - Proverbs 3:5 KJV

If you are not comfortable in the position that you are in now, know what you can achieve if you put your fears aside and push forward. Learn how to walk by faith and not by sight. You were born to succeed. God put you here for a reason, not to stay in the same position as you have been in for years. Live with expectancy that God is going to make improvements in your life. God is ready to give you a plan to make you move in a different direction. He is ready to make changes in your life. He is ready to prepare you for greater things. God is ready to anoint you with His power and authority for the harvest. So, get ready to walk into your SEASON!

_____
_____
_____
_____
_____

STORM & SOLUTIONS PEARLS

"I will praise thee; for I am fearfully and wonderfully made: marvellous are thy works; and that my soul knoweth right well." - Psalm 139:14 KJV

Nothing is greater than being yourself. Everybody else is already taken. Be who you are, show who you are, and never be afraid to let the world see you shine. You are special, beautiful, and can do anything you put your mind to do. It all starts with the right decision to try because without trying you will never find out who you are. Take the initiative, move forward and you will see the results. Be positive, confident, stand tall, smile, enjoy, be kind and you will start seeing life in a different and better way. Always remember if things are not going the way you planned, keep going. Never give up. Take a different route. There is a road that will lead you to where you want to be and where you should be. Have faith and believe in yourself.

STORM & SOLUTIONS PEARLS

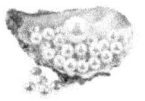

"I will instruct thee and teach thee in the way which thou shalt go: I will guide thee with mine eye." - Psalm 32:8 KJV

There are things that God will do before he opens doors for us. God prepares us from the inside, because it would not do any good if we are not prepared to handle the blessing, He has in store for us. So, before God opens any door in our life, He looks at the areas in our life that we need to work on and so that we can perfect it. Another thing that God will do is place people in our lives for the perfection of His plan. It may not be who we think we need, but God knows who we need and why He placed them within our lives. God wants the best for us. He wants to give us a life that He knows will be fulfilling to us. He wants us to grow into the person He wants us to be. When God sees you are doing your part, developing what he has given you, then He will do His part and open that door that no man can shut.

STORM & SOLUTIONS PEARLS

> "But without faith it is impossible to please him: for he that cometh to God must believe that he is, and that he is a rewarder of them that diligently seek him."
> Hebrews 11:6 KJV

God may be calling you to do something and you are afraid to leave your comfort zone. It can be scary to step out and do something that God has called you to do. Many times, God's plan for us causes us to face our fears. Maybe you have a fear of speaking in public, singing a solo in from of a crowd, praying out loud, afraid to drive, sharing a testimony, etc. Sometimes when God calls us to do something and it terrifies us and we ignore His call, remember that in your weakness he is strong. He will strengthen you and enable you. He is waiting for you to step out on faith, wherein you must rely solely on Him ...and he will meet you there. When you put your faith in Him, rest assure he will show up.

God uses some who are confident in themselves but, He also uses those who say:

"I can't do it, I'm not worthy, I don't have what it takes, I'm afraid to take that leap"...because when they do His power is shown through them. God is not limited by our weakness and inabilities. True faith in God requires us to step out on His strength in the absence of our own abilities. If God calls you to do it, you cannot and will not fail. Just step out on Faith and watch God work in your life!!

STORM & SOLUTIONS PEARLS

"Hast thou not known? hast thou not heard, that the everlasting God, the Lord, the Creator of the ends of the earth, fainteth not, neither is weary? there is no searching of his understanding. He giveth power to the faint; and to them that have no might he increaseth strength. Even the youths shall faint and be weary, and the young men shall utterly fall: But they that wait upon the Lord shall renew their strength; they shall mount up with wings as eagles; they shall run, and not be weary; and they shall walk, and not faint."
Isaiah 40:28-31 KJV

There is one statement that will always hold true. If God brings you to it, he will bring you through it. If you feel like you're in the fire today and the heat is being turned up and it seems as if everything is coming against you, let me encourage you, it's because there is something GREAT in store. When the heat gets turned up, it means you're close to your breakthrough. God is with you when you are in the fire. If you stay in faith and keep your eyes focused on Him in prayer and in praise, He will do for you what he did for the 3 Hebrew boys; Shadrach, Meshach and Abednego. He'll bring you through the fire – even without smelling like smoke – Into something greater than what you asked of Him.

Therefore, if you position yourself to be in a place where God is the center of your JOY, rest assured you are in the safest place to be. He will see you through your difficult journey in life every step of the way. If you are not, take hold of His hand on today and stay in Faith and Trust Him. Let Him bring you through that situation you are in and every other situation you may go through. Your Greater is Coming!

STORM & SOLUTIONS PEARLS

STORM & SOLUTIONS PEARLS

"Trust in the LORD with all thine heart; and lean not unto thine own understanding. In all thy ways acknowledge him, and he shall direct thy paths." - Proverbs 3:5-6 KJV

"God loves us too much to promote us before we are ready"

In the midst of going through, it's for a reason. Stop listening to the devil and letting him guide you on what you need to do, trying to give you a quick fix on your situation. God wants to guide us on what we need to do. He will remove us from our comfort zone so that we can solely rely on Him. God wants us to trust Him and make us strong for the remarkable blessings He is about to pour on us. He allows the path to be difficult sometimes because His intentions are to refine us. He allows the path to be difficult sometimes because His intentions are to refine us and prepare us to do and to go where He wants us to go. If we don't have God in our life, we will miss out on all the blessings He has in store for us. For true happiness and a wonderful life, let us surrender our life to God.

STORM & SOLUTIONS PEARLS

"It is better to trust in the LORD than to put confidence in man." - Psalm 118:8 KJV

If their name isn't God, their opinion doesn't matter, and their approval is not needed

If someone doubts you and tells you that you can't do something, keep in mind they are speaking from within the boundaries of their limitations. In this world of doubters that's trying to make you like them we should not let the opinions of others influence us. You have realistic goals in mind and God has given you the 'courage to step up and pursue them.' When these doubters laugh at you for being different...laugh at them for never trying.

_____
_____
_____
_____

STORM & SOLUTIONS PEARLS

"Casting all your care upon him; he careth for you." - I Peter 5:7 KJV

"You cannot go forward when you keep looking in the rearview mirror!"- Dan Quinn

Don't stop now!! Your breakthrough is ahead of you. The last mile is usually the hardest one... so keep moving forward and stop looking back, your blessing is ahead. God is about to do something BIG! Continue to believe in God and He will bring victory. Strengthen your Faith to believe that ALL things are possible.

_____

_____

_____

_____

_____

_____

_____

STORM & SOLUTIONS PEARLS

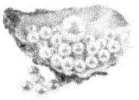

"Fear thou not; for I am with thee: be not dismayed; for I am thy God: I will strengthen thee; yea, I will help thee; yea, I will uphold thee with the right hand of my righteousness."
- Isaiah 41:10 KJV

Before I accept Christ in my Life, I was headed down the path of destruction and I knew I needed someone to guide me in the right direction. I knew I had to give up all the partying and drinking. I needed guidance in my life. I knew I needed to talk to someone about my situation. I confided in my sister and we talked for a while. She told me prayer was the first place I needed to start. She told me to keep calling on God in prayer and she gave me my first bible to read.

God showed me exactly how to live a Godly life. Through prayer, putting my trust in Him whole heartedly and believing on Him for guidance. I put my trust and belief in His hands. God didn't give me the people I wanted in my life, instead He gave me the people I needed to teach me, to lead me, to love me and to make me exactly the way He wanted me to be. The most amazing thing about God is that He will put the right people in your path who belong in your life right at the moment you were about to give up. Sometimes they are there for that moment just to get you through and sometimes they are there for a lifetime. Trust me, God knows who is temporary and whom He wants to stay.

_____
_____
_____
_____
_____
_____
_____
_____
_____
_____
_____
_____
_____

STORM & SOLUTIONS PEARLS

"But without faith it is impossible to please him: for he that cometh to God must believe that he is, and that he is a rewarder of them that diligently seek him."
- Hebrews 11:6 KJV

God may be calling you to do something and you are afraid to leave your comfort zone. It can be scary to step out and do something that God has called you to do. Many times, God's plan for us causes us to face our fears. Maybe you have a fear of speaking in public, singing a solo in from of a crowd, praying out loud, afraid to drive, sharing a testimony, etc. Sometimes when God calls us to do something and it terrifies us and we ignore His call, remember that in your weakness he is strong. He will strengthen you and enable you.

He is waiting for you to step out on faith, wherein you must rely solely on Him...and he will meet you there. When you put your faith in Him, rest assure he will show up. God uses some who are confident in themselves but, He also uses those who say:

"I can't do it, I'm not worthy, I don't have what it takes,

STORM & SOLUTIONS PEARLS

I'm afraid to take that leap"...because when they do His power is shown through them. God is not limited by our weakness and inabilities. True faith in God requires us to step out on His strength in the absence of our own abilities.

If God calls you to do it, you cannot and will not fail. Just step out on Faith and watch God work in your life!!

STORM & SOLUTIONS PEARLS

STORM & SOLUTIONS PEARLS

"For I know the thoughts that I think toward you, saith the LORD, thoughts of peace, and not of evil, to give you an expected end." - Jeremiah 29:11 KJV

Never doubt the struggle because at the end it may just be a celebration!!

God already knows how many times we will fall and stumble during our journey. He already knows what our struggles will be, and who or what will cause us to trip during our walk-in life. So, when we have these moments, He wants us to seek His face wholeheartedly. He wants us to trust and believe in Him and know that He will bring us out of ALL situations. Spend time with God, get to know him.

Create a personal relationship with Him… then you will know that when you go through setbacks or when people intentionally overlook you for the work you have done; God is busy working behind the scenes. You might not see the outcome of your struggles now, but further down the road you will know it was God who made it all possible for you to be successful. Never underestimate God's ability,

He has a plan for your life. Read His Word!!!

Pearls of Motivation

Proverbs 3:5-6 KJV

Trust in the LORD with all thine heart; and lean not unto thine own understanding. In all thy ways acknowledge him, and he shall direct thy paths.

"But without faith it is impossible to please him: for he that cometh to God must believe that he is, and that he is a rewarder of them that diligently seek him."
- Hebrews 11:6 KJV

God may be calling you to do something for Him and you are afraid to leave your comfort zone. It can be scary to step out and do something that God called you to do. Many times, God's plan for us causes us to face our fears. Maybe you have a fear of speaking in public, singing in front of a crowd, praying out loud, sharing a testimony, etc. Sometimes when God calls us to do something it is terrifying, and we do not heed His call. Just know that in your weakness He is strong, if He calls you to do it, He will strengthen you and enable you. He is waiting for you to step out on faith, wherein you must rely solely on him... and he will meet you there. When you put your faith in Him, rest assured He will show up. God uses some who are confident in themselves but, He also uses those who say: "I can't do it, I'm not worthy, I don't have what it takes, I'm afraid to take that leap"... because when they do, His power is shone through them.

God is not limited by our weaknesses and inabilities. True Faith in God requires us to step out on His strength in the absence of our inabilities. If God calls you to do it, you cannot fail. Just step out on Faith!!

MOTIVATION PEARLS

MOTIVATION PEARLS

"For every man shall bear his own burden."
- Galatians 6:5 KJV

Accept responsibility for your life. Know that it is you who will get you to where you want to go, no one else. Put yourself above the negative comments of others. Do not listen to them. Do not let your dreams be impacted by the words of others. Make your dreams a reality. Be patient. Be hopeful. It may look a little dim now... but no matter how dark the night gets, daybreak will follow. Never settle for ordinary, be extraordinary. Be the main character in your own story. Know your self-worth that is the only way you will know who you are. Greatness is in you; you are a child of the Most High God... Claim it!

_____

_____

_____

_____

_____

_____

MOTIVATION PEARLS

MOTIVATION PEARLS

"I can do all things through Christ which strengtheneth me."
- Philippians 4:13 KJV

Some journeys are meant to be taken alone. I have been allowed to walk away from people who were hindrances to my life. They helped me to develop tough skin and determination to go at it alone without their support. It was my time to declutter. I came to know that I am the master of my vision. I came to trust in God and lean on my faith for His guidance. The door to your journey is opening and your life too will be changed forever. You are a leaper and You shall go forth!! You cannot wait! You will, You must, and You shall...

MOTIVATION PEARLS

"For the joy of the Lord is my strength."
- Nehemiah 8:10 KJV

I will begin today by controlling my thoughts. I want to be happy. Therefore, I will have thoughts that are happy and hopeful. I will not let petty things such as long lines in the grocery stores, long waits at the doctor's office and complaining about the things I cannot control replace my joy. I will avoid negative talk and gossip. I will be hopeful and confident in my goals, and victory will be my success. Time is precious; therefore, I refuse to allow what time I have to be used feeling sorry for myself and being fearful. I will face this day thanking God for allowing me to see another day and the courage to go out to face the world. I will take in every minute as though it is my last. When tomorrow comes, today will be gone forever. While it is here, I will use it for loving, caring, and giving. I will not let past failures haunt me. Even though my life is scarred with mistakes, I refuse to think back and wonder about my failures. I will admit them. I will correct them. I will press on victoriously. Failure never killed anyone. It is okay to fall; I will get up. It is okay to fail, I will succeed. I will spend time with those I love. You can own the world but lack love. You can have nothing but be wealthy in your relationship. Today I will spend time with those special people in my life. I will spend that quiet time with God. I will spend quality time with my spouse, my children, and my friends. Starting today no one will ever steal my JOY!!

MOTIVATION PEARLS

MOTIVATION PEARLS

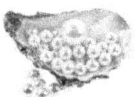

"Be still and know that I am God: I will be exalted among the heathen, I will be exalted in the earth."
- Psalm 46:10 KJV

Declare today that you will not stress over things that you cannot control. People will be people, jobs will be jobs, but one thing is for sure, GOD is still GOD!! Let Him handle it. So, stop stressing.

MOTIVATION PEARLS

"Remember ye not the former things, neither consider the things of old. Behold, I will do a new thing; now it shall spring forth; shall ye not know it? I will even make a way in the wilderness, and rivers in the desert."
- Isaiah 43:18-19 KJV

There comes a time in your life when for different reasons it is necessary to let things go. So, the moment you hear God clearly say "Stop waiting for them to catch up... go forth. Fasten your seat belt prepare for takeoff. I am taking you to the next level! Prepare yourself for the trip. You may have to sacrifice friends, but the trip will be well worth it. The takeoff may be a little bumpy along the way, but when you let go and follow my directions... The landing will be amazing!!"

_____

_____

_____

_____

_____

_____

_____

MOTIVATION PEARLS

"Therefore if any man be in Christ, he is a new creature: old things are passed away; behold, all things are become new." - 2 Corinthians 5:17 KJV

Today is a new day. Do not let your past interfere with your future. Let today be the day you stop being a victim of your past and start actively taking steps towards the life you want. You have the power and the time to turn your life around. Take control of your life and embrace the truth of your greatness. You were created in the image of God and we know God to be awesome. You were not meant to have an average life... you were created to have an awesome life! Your only limit is you.

Your past cannot be changed; Do not allow your past to keep reminding you of who you were. God's Truth gives us a new identity and enables us to be transformed! We are a new creation and no longer condemned of past sins. Move on to be the person God created you to be and walk in the newness of your life!

MOTIVATION PEARLS

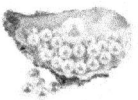

"O give thanks unto the Lord; for he is good; for his mercy endureth for ever." - 1 Chronicles 16:34 KJV

**"God smiles when we praise and thank Him continually. Few things feel better than receiving heartfelt praise and appreciation from someone else. God loves it, too... an amazing thing happens when we offer praise and thanksgiving to God. When we give God enjoyment, our hearts are filled with joy."
- Rick Warren**

Are you thankful for your present circumstances? Are you thankful for the life God has given you, for your Family, for your Pastor, for your Church family, for your salvation, or your job? Being thankful is the key that turns your situation around because it changes you, your outlook on things, and your attitude. There is power in a thankful heart. So, thank God for all the blessings He has given you instead of dwelling on the negative. Thank Him for the difficulties. It may be hard to do, but He can turn your troubles into triumphs. During the difficult times be very careful to watch your tongue. Instead of complaining, think of ways you can verbally offer God praise. Do not wish that your life was different. God knows what is best. When we begin to thank God for what we have rather than comparing ourselves with others, it opens the door for God's blessings to us. Whenever we give thanks to God, even though our difficult circumstances, watch the blessings flow. So, bring pleasure to God's heart; smile, and thank Him. Then sit back and watch God change things.

MOTIVATION PEARLS

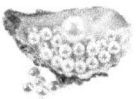

"And let us not be weary in well doing: for in due season we shall reap, if we faint not." - Galatians 6:9 KJV

Life is going to throw you some curve balls sometimes. But remember: Every time you take a step backward, get up and take two steps forward. Fall seven times, stand up eight.

Never give up. Every step, no matter how small, is a step in the right direction. Then you will realize all the things you used to trip over; you can walk over now! This week make that curveball a home run... hit it out of the park!!

_____
_____
_____
_____
_____
_____
_____

MOTIVATION PEARLS

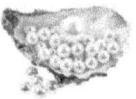

"God is our refuge and strength, a very present help in trouble. Therefore will not we fear, though the earth be removed, and though the mountains be carried into the midst of the sea;" - Psalm 46:1-2 KJV

This is for all the people who choose to shine even after all the storms they have been through are over. You have faced many challenges and struggles in your life and you still have the power to push on. Your courage speaks for itself. Keep persevering and your goal is within reach. Keep praying and thanking God for all your struggles. Once the storm is over, you will not remember how you made it through, how you manage to survive. But one thing is for certain, when you come out of the storm, you will not be the same. That is what storms are all about. This allows you to become that which you aspire to be and much better. Your courage speaks volumes. When you look back on your life, you see pain, mistakes, and heartaches. When you look in the mirror, you see strength, learned lessons, and pride in yourself. Always remember, you have made it this far and you can make it through whatever comes next. Keep shining.

MOTIVATION PEARLS

MOTIVATION PEARLS

"And be not conformed to this world: but be ye transformed by the renewing of your mind, that ye may prove what is that good, and acceptable, and perfect, will of God." -Romans 12:2 KJV

There will be many chapters in your life. Do not get lost in the one you are in now. I know it is so much easier for us to focus on the storm than it is for us to focus on the rainbow. But focusing on the storm keeps us fearful and stuck. The storm is dark and unpredictable so therefore we are stuck in that situation. Know that God knows your strengths and weaknesses and can plan so that you can turn the page in your life to the next chapter He has prepared you for. The rainbow is beautiful, vibrant, and promising and it always shows up after the storm so there is hope. Change your thinking and you will change your life. Turn that page!!

_____
_____
_____
_____

MOTIVATION PEARLS

MOTIVATION PEARLS

"A time to get, and a time to lose; a time to keep, and a time to cast away" - Ecclesiastes 3:6 KJV

Letting go is difficult, but it's something we constantly have to do as we live from one day to the next, it's adjusting to a situation in this changing world we live in, leaving behind the old to make way for the new. There are many reasons we may want to let go sooner rather than later.

Maybe someone wants you to be someone you are not. Maybe you had your trust and your heart broken too many times by the same person. Or maybe you have simply been living a lifestyle that makes you unhappy. There may be endless possibilities. The idea of letting go can seem hard, but it can be done by using the right approach from an effective point of view. One way and the best way is to pray and put it in God's hands. Secondly, think of something positive and wonderful that you want to happen, pray about it and make it happen. Third, write down all the difficulties in your life, pray over them, then torch them... think of it as closure in your life.

MOTIVATION PEARLS

Let's stop thinking and start doing. We need to take this advice, make it happen, and use it.

MOTIVATION PEARLS

"For thou, Lord, wilt bless the righteous; with favour wilt thou compass him as with a shield." - Psalm 5:12 KJV

We give Him our heart; He gives us life. He gives us love, even when we do not deserve it. When we feel so all alone, He comforts and consoles us. When we have spent all, He restores all and more. When we choose the wrong path, He guides us in the right direction. Some may call it luck, but we know it is "God's Favor" That's why we live to worship Him.

_____
_____
_____
_____
_____
_____
_____
_____
_____
_____

Faith Pearls that Change Doubts into Beliefs

Matthew 21:21

Jesus answered and said unto them, Verily I say unto you, If ye have faith, and doubt not, ye shall not only do this which is done to the fig tree, but also if ye shall say unto this mountain, Be thou removed, and be thou cast into the sea; it shall be done.

"Grant thee according to thine own heart, and fulfil all thy counsel. We will rejoice in thy salvation, and in the name of our God we will set up our banners: the Lord fulfil all thy petitions. Now know I that the Lord saveth his anointed; he will hear him from his holy heaven with the saving strength of his right hand." - Psalms 20:4-6 KJV

Most people put limits on themselves. You can accomplish anything you set your mind on. There may be people out there that will try to tell you that you can't and tell you it's impossible. You will have some you think are friends, who say your dreams are too big and your hopes are too high. These are people who don't want you to accomplish anything, and to stay on their level.

Step up your game and surround yourself with people who believe in you, people whose expectations reach above and beyond or by people who will help open doors of opportunities for you... "the sky is not the limit... you are!!"

What you believe... you can achieve!!!

FAITH PEARLS

FAITH PEARLS

"And the Lord, he it is that doth go before thee; he will be with thee, he will not fail thee, neither forsake thee: fear not, neither be dismayed." - Deuteronomy 31:8 KJV

You cannot live your life in fear. Your fears do not control you unless you allow them. The devil is not as powerful as you think. If you are constantly feeling as though you are in the fight of your life, you are going against God's plan for you. Fear will cause us to settle for less than God's best. Stand still and let God fight your battle. Give it to Him and you will find true peace. When you are no longer a slave to fear, the devil will flee. Go where there is love and peace, and that is with God. Do not let your fears destroy your journey to success in life.

_____

_____

_____

_____

_____

FAITH PEARLS

FAITH PEARLS

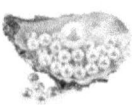

"The righteous cry, and the Lord heareth, and delivereth them out of all their troubles." - Psalm 34:17 KJV

When you are at your lowest and you can still praise God... watch those storms cease!!! Some of your wonderful blessings come when you are going through trials. We need to trust Him in all circumstances. We touch the heart of God when we praise and love Him amid trouble. That is the beauty of God's gift!!!

FAITH PEARLS

"And he said unto me, My grace is sufficient for thee: for my strength is made perfect in weakness. Most gladly therefore will I rather glory in my infirmities, that the power of Christ may rest upon me." - II Corinthians 12:9 KJV

God has proven to us in many ways that his grace is more than enough to see us through our trials. He has opened doors of opportunity and He will see us through any new challenges that may come our way. We tend to believe that nothing is happening if we do not see change.

Instead of praying for God to do what we think is best or to remove stumbling blocks from our lives, we should pray for God's grace and understand that His grace is sufficient. Instead of focusing on circumstances, we need to rejoice in the gift of God's grace and to keep our focus on how big God is.

God's grace means that because of His mercy, He is able to forgive and still love us despite our shortcomings. Putting it simply, grace can be defined as God's unmerited favor. Grace also means getting from God what we do not deserve. Grace is the power of God to do for us what we cannot do for ourselves. Grace, that is why it is called Amazing!!

FAITH PEARLS

"After these things the word of the Lord came unto Abram in a vision, saying, Fear not, Abram: I am thy shield, and thy exceeding great reward." - Genesis 15:1 KJV

When God is about to show you the vision, He has for you to promote the talents and goals in your life be ready to step out on faith. That is when the enemy will try to throw up roadblocks or cloud your mind with negative thoughts. He will even try to tempt you to change your goals. But if we remember to keep our focus on God there is nothing the enemy can do to persuade us not to reach our destiny that has been determined by God. Our God is an awesome God. He wants to overwhelm us with His goodness so that we can be successful.

_____

_____

_____

_____

_____

_____

FAITH PEARLS

"I will instruct thee and teach thee in the way which thou shalt go: I will guide thee with mine eye." - Psalm 32:8 KJV

Sometimes your plan does not work, because God has a better plan. When it seems, there is no way out...that's when God shows you the plan that He has for you!! That is how He does it!! God is AWESOME!!

_____

_____

_____

_____

_____

_____

_____

_____

_____

_____

"He that covereth his sins shall not prosper: but whoso confesseth and forsaketh them shall have mercy." - Proverbs 28:13 KJV

Strangely, so many people think it shows weakness for you to admit your mistakes, and say you are sorry. In truth, it is a sign of both strength and wisdom. Asking forgiveness helps us to learn, to grow, and to love. It brings us closer to the blessings God has for us. It helps us to become the person God wants us to be. It is those who never say they are sorry who end up living a troubled life. God has promised us peace when we think about the right things. Dwelling on past hurts and unpleasant situations can hurt your present. What God is doing for you is greater than what anyone has done to you.

_____

_____

_____

_____

_____

_____

FAITH PEARLS

"But thanks be to God, which giveth us the victory through our Lord Jesus Christ." - 1 Corinthians 15:57 KJV

There is one thing that can prevent you from reaching your victory and that is your fear of trusting and totaling surrendering to God. Take authority over anything that keeps you from God's best. Fear is not of God. It is designed to keep you from moving to your destiny and keep you from receiving all that God has for you. God has armed you with His Word... use this powerful weapon against the enemy daily! Read the Word, Speak the Word, Act on the Word, then watch God's plan for your life overcome any obstacle that comes your way- VICTORY will be yours!!

_____
_____
_____
_____
_____
_____
_____

Pearls of Gratitude

Psalms 23 KJV

The Lord is my shepherd; I shall not want. He maketh me to lie down in green pastures: he leadeth me beside the still waters.

He restoreth my soul: he leadeth me in the paths of righteousness for his name's sake.

Yea, though I walk through the valley of the shadow of death, I will fear no evil: for thou art with me; thy rod and thy staff they comfort me.

Thou preparest a table before me in the presence of mine enemies: thou anointest my head with oil; my cup runneth over.

Surely goodness and mercy shall follow me all the days of my life: and I will dwell in the house of the Lord for ever.

"Blessed is the man that endureth temptation: for when he is tried, he shall receive the crown of life, which the Lord hath promised to them that love him." -James 1:12. KJV

"Don't give up! It is not over. Every set-back bears with it the seeds of a come-back." Steve Maraboli

You will never experience life if you do not have a setback, you will never learn to be successful if you don't taste failure. Failure is a learning experience. If we give-up we will never learn from our mistakes. You are the success you are today by the mistakes God helped you correct on yesterday. Remember: The Setback you experienced is a Setup for a greater Comeback!! Be a bounce-back person!! Do not let setbacks be an obstacle in your life. Move forward to your success! Be informed ... God did not put you here to fail!

_____

_____

_____

_____

_____

GRATITUDE PEARLS

GRATITUDE PEARLS

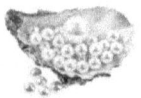

"This is the day which the Lord has made; we will rejoice and be glad in it." - Psalm 118:24 KJV

When you open your eyes in the morning, everything is fresh and new before you start your day. Each new day is another gift from God that He has given you. It is up to you to determine what your day will be like. You can make it a fresh beginning to choose love, create joy, spread laughter, help others, and give something back to the world. Each moment is another chance to share a hug, a smile, a compliment, or an act of kindness. It does not matter how many mistakes you made in the past, wrong turns you have taken or the days you have wasted. We all can begin again this morning. God is there waiting to help us live this day, to share the love, and help others who are in need. There is an old saying that goes, "if you wake up breathing, you still have another chance." Do not waste your chance today. Make your fresh start now. Wake up every morning and say, "Good Morning God! Thank you for my life!" Then go out and live it in joy, love, and oneness with Him. Open your heart, soul, and mind to the love, goodness, and delight that is all around you. Share all

GRATITUDE PEARLS

the wonderful talent, compassion, and helpfulness that is within you with others. And make each new day a fresh start to live and spread love.

"In every thing give thanks: for this is the will of God in Christ Jesus concerning you." - I Thessalonians 5:18 KJV

Take a few minutes today to thank God for the things in your life for which you are truly grateful. Sometimes we get so caught up in the heat of the battles we are facing that all of our thoughts, prayers, and attention are focused on the battles only. And when we get so caught up, we stop giving thanks to the wonderful God we serve and all He has done in the past for us, which can lead down a road of destruction and unbelief. Do not wait to give thanks to God when we see the answers to our prayers. Give thanks to Him upfront for what we have been given and trust him to take the next step. Come to Him today with your prayers. Come to Him with Thanksgiving in your heart. Thank Him for those things in your life for which you are truly grateful, for those things that may be hard to accept right now, and watch God use them for your good, for the answers to your prayers that haven't happened yet, but by your faith, you will believe it will come in a way that goes beyond all you can ask or imagine. Let God renew your mind by giving thanks to Him.

GRATITUDE PEARLS

GRATITUDE PEARLS

"Make a joyful noise unto the Lord, all ye lands. Serve the Lord with gladness: come before his presence with singing. Know ye that the Lord he is God: it is he that hath made us, and not we ourselves; we are his people, and the sheep of his pasture. Enter into his gates with thanksgiving, and into his courts with praise: be thankful unto him, and bless his name. For the Lord is good; his mercy is everlasting; and his truth endureth to all generations." - Psalms 100:1-5 KJV

It is a challenge to grow up with a thankful heart. From an early age we are exposed to complainers, grumblers, criticizers, and opinionated people. We complain about the weather, traffic, food, work, neighbors, bills, the government, church, and life in general. Worst of all we even complain about God. How can we who have received so much be so ungrateful? God is not happy with us. The Spirit and the joy of the Lord within us is diminished. Being thankful sweetens us, grumbling sours us; being thankful brings sunshine to our appearance, being ungrateful casts a shadow; being thankful brings a melody to our spirit, criticism makes us sound off-key; being thankful keeps our feet on, the road to success, complaints take us down the road to failure. When our

GRATITUDE PEARLS

hearts are filled with gratefulness we may feel as if our thanksgiving is adequate of what God wants. The heart of God will be overjoyed to hear that your heartfelt thanks is being given freely to Him.

GRATITUDE PEARLS

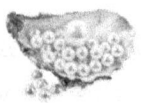

"Take therefore no thought for the morrow: for the morrow shall take thought for the things of itself. Sufficient unto the day is the evil thereof." - Matthew 6:34 KJV

Do not worry about tomorrow because the same God who planned your day today has already planned it for tomorrow. Try giving your entire attention to what God is doing right now, and do not get worked up about what may or may not happen tomorrow. God will help you deal with whatever hard things come up when the time comes. He already knows. So, do not try to help Him plan your tomorrow it's already done!!

_____
_____
_____
_____
_____
_____
_____
_____

GRATITUDE PEARLS

"That, according as it is written, He that glorieth, let him glory in the Lord." - I Corinthians 1:31 KJV

Today I am speaking of the wonderful things my God has done. God woke me up this morning!! God is so great; He even looks after me. God has been with me all my days and I am happy because he is my friend, my strength, and my place of comfort. That is how great MY GOD is!! So today, look for ways to brag on your God. If you are breathing today, brag on Him as your Creator. If you got to your destination safely today, brag on Him for being your Protector. If you are facing a difficulty, brag on the fact that He is your Deliverer and He will bring you out of it. Keep declaring and bragging on His goodness and faithfulness and watch how God works in you.

We serve an AWESOME GOD!!

GRATITUDE PEARLS

GRATITUDE PEARLS

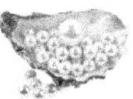

"And let the beauty of the Lord our God be upon us: and establish thou the work of our hands upon us; yea, the work of our hands establish thou it." - Psalms 90:17 KJV

Because you are highly favored in God, during impossible situations you will experience great victories, turnarounds, and breakthroughs like never before. You will receive recognition and promotions. You will win battles that you do not even have to lift a finger to fight. Because of God's favor the enemy cannot even win. Your finances will increase. Everything that the devil stole from you will be restored. Every setback you experience will be a setup for a miraculous comeback. Every bad break, every disappointment, every person that did you wrong was a part of His plan to get you to where you are supposed to be. Get ready for all the blessings God has in store for you! God's favor will surround you like a shield, everything that is not in His plan for you will bounce off.

_____

_____

_____

_____

GRATITUDE PEARLS

GRATITUDE PEARLS

"The Lord is my rock, and my fortress, and my deliverer; my God, my strength, in whom I will trust; my buckler, and the horn of my salvation, and my high tower." - Psalms 18:2 KJV

Despite the pain, the highest level of worship is praising God. We should thank God during the trials, trust Him when we are tempted to lose hope and love Him when He seems so far away. At your lowest He is your Hope, at your darkest God is your Light, at your weakest God is your Strength and at your saddest God is your Comforter. God is your All and All!

_____

_____

_____

_____

_____

_____

_____

_____

_____

"And we know that all things work together for good to them that love God, to them who are the called according to his purpose." - Romans 8:28 KJV

If your life is not all that you hoped it would be, it is the result of your negative thoughts that have attracted you to the things that you do not want, while overlooking the positive things you greatly crave for. Focus clearly on your purpose in life. Write the vision, make it plain, and then act upon it. You know the expectations and hopes you have for your life. If you want success, riches, and love in life then your current thoughts and situation must change.

_____

_____

_____

_____

_____

_____

_____

_____

GRATITUDE PEARLS

"I am crucified with Christ: nevertheless I live; yet not I, but Christ liveth in me: and the life which I now live in the flesh I live by the faith of the Son of God, who loved me, and gave himself for me." - Galatians 2:20 KJV

Let every day be a dream you can wake up and touch because of your creation. Let every day be a moment you can feel, because your hands made this dream come to pass. Let every day be a reason to live, because life is too short to be negative... Life will just not wait for us to live. We are in it now and now is the time to live it. Today create your sunshine and let the warmth revive you! Be thankful for every day God has given you life. Commit to living your life the way God wants you to live it. Love the life you live!

_____

_____

_____

_____

_____

_____

_____

_____

"And whatsoever ye do, do it heartily, as to the Lord, and not unto men;" - Colossians 3:23 KJV

Today is your day to dust off God's promises to you and put them to work! It is time to put your fears to rest. Your days of doubt are gone. Your work for the Lord has been put off long enough! God has placed a wonderful purpose within you. Over the years, you have been slowly discovering who you are and who God has called you to be. You have learned that you are determined to do these things but at your own pace. Today is the day that God is calling you to take charge of your life. Today is the day that you have learned that you are worthy of God's promises and that God's plan for you is the best. You will learn more about yourself in this season than at any other time in your life. You will now understand that the things that you were putting off was necessary, but it was for you to continue to grow and develop for this time. You are now ready to go forth!! This is the time to move and to strive. Your door is open! Walk through it in Faith!

_____

_____

_____

GRATITUDE PEARLS

GRATITUDE PEARLS

"For we are his workmanship, created in Christ Jesus unto good works, which God hath before ordained that we should walk in them." - Ephesians 2:10 KJV

Nothing is greater than being yourself. You are a masterpiece! When God made you, He did break the mold. There is no other person who is exactly like you. You are an original. He made you special, so be who you are, show who you are, and never be afraid to shine. You can do anything you put your mind to do. Remember God had a purpose in mind for us even before we came into being. Stay positive, be confident, smile, be kind, move forward, and start living your way in a Godly manner, and you will start seeing life differently and great things will start to happen in your life. There is a road that will take you to where He wants you to be and where you ought to be. You may not be there yet; just have faith and believe in yourself. Remember your plan may not be the plan God has for you. Pray for direction in your life and watch God change things.

_____
_____
_____

GRATITUDE PEARLS

"Rejoicing in hope; patient in tribulation; continuing instant in prayer;" - I Corinthians 2:9 KJV

God puts dreams in our hearts to prepare us for greater things, and if we trust Him enough to take Him at His word, we will find ourselves fulfilling those dreams. Unfortunately, the path that takes us to fulfill those dreams is sometimes blocked by obstacles. Nothing worth having ever comes easy or quickly. Sometimes we have to wait until God reveals it to us. Storms will come and we will have doubts. God allows the path to be difficult because He intends to refine us and prepare us for what He promised. The enemy puts obstacles in our path, but God intends to strengthen us and lead us. When the storm is over and your dream has become a reality, then you can look back and realize that the trials that you went through were really necessary. You received a better blessing than what you hoped for.

_____

_____

_____

_____

GRATITUDE PEARLS

GRATITUDE PEARLS

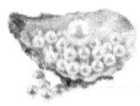

"Delight thyself also in the Lord: and he shall give thee the desires of thine heart." - Psalms 37:4 KJV

Keep your dreams alive. To achieve anything requires faith, belief in yourself, a vision, hard work, determination, and dedication. Remember all things are possible for those who believe. Don't underestimate your worth by comparing yourself to others. We are special because each of us is different. The greatest step of your success in life will not be that you finally finished, it will be that you dared to begin. Bring your dreams to life! Believe in yourself!!!

The only thing that will stop you from fulfilling your dreams is you!!

_____
_____
_____
_____
_____
_____
_____

GRATITUDE PEARLS

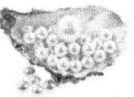

"Do all things without murmurings and disputings:"
- Philippians 2:14 KJV

I cried because I had no shoes... then I met a man who had no feet! - Mahatma Gandhi

You've heard people say:

Today is a terrible day for me, everything that can go wrong is going wrong. Well, let us examine that statement.

First, you woke up this morning; therefore, you are still alive. You still have a place to live and food on the table. You have clothes on your back and shoes on your feet. You still have water, electricity, fairly good health, and the use of all your limbs. Today is a great day for you! You are a super blessed child of God!! Let's take a moment to think before we start complaining and thank God for another day!!!!

_____

_____

_____

_____

GRATITUDE PEARLS

ABOUT THE AUTHOR

 Born in Durham North Carolina, Precisus LaWarn Curry is the ninth child out of eleven children. At an early age, she loved reading books that would stretch beyond her imagination and inspire her to be an encouragement to others. Pearls of Wisdom is an extension of what she does on a daily basis.

She gave her life to Christ, January 13, 1993. She is a born-again Christian, baptized and filled with the Holy Ghost. She was quoted as saying, "Knowing Jesus is my rock, I can do all things through Him."

Her goal is to introduce nonbelievers to Christ. To let them know what an awesome God she serves. No matter how bad a situation may seem, He is the only one that can change it. She quoted, "I think God is using me to speak through my book to the nonbelievers and to encourage the believers that God is the Truth, the Way, and the Light. (John 14:6 KJV). And for this I am grateful!!"

Connect with Precisus on:
Facebook: @ pregal.barbee
Email: precisusbarbee@gmail.com

www.ingramcontent.com/pod-product-compliance
Lightning Source LLC
Chambersburg PA
CBHW062000070426
42450CB00025BA/1300